The Queen of
SHEBA

Copyright © Hood Hood Books
First published 1996
Reprinted 2003

Hood Hood Books
46 Clabon Mews
London SW1X OEH

Tel: 44 20 7584 7878
Fax: 44 20 7225 0386
E-Mail: info@hoodhood.com
Website: www.hoodhood.com

British Library Cataloguing–in–Publication Data
A catalogue record for this book is available from the British Library

ISBN 1 900251 11 6

No part of this book may be reproduced
in any form without permission of the publishers.
All rights reserved.

Origination by Fine Line Graphics - London
Printed by IPH - Egypt

THE QUEEN OF SHEBA

Written by
MARION KHALIDI

&

Illustrated by
AHMED JABIR

THE QUEEN OF
SHEBA

LONG AGO IN THE CITY OF JERUSALEM lived the great Prophet, King Solomon. He commanded a large, powerful army whose cavalry alone numbered 12,000 horses and 400 chariots, but since he was a fair and good King he ruled peacefully over the land and his subjects were happy and content.

King Solomon was blessed by God with the gifts of wisdom and intelligence. He controlled the wind that blew across the land at his will and ruled over the demons and Jinns who worked in his service building bridges and temples. (The Jinns are creatures from the spirit world made of smokeless fire). King Solomon could also understand and speak the language of animals and birds.

One day he called to all the birds of heaven, all the beasts of the field and all the creatures that crawled on the earth and ordered them to come before him. When they heard the King's command, every animal - from the noble lion to the lowly ant - gathered at his throne. But when Solomon looked around, he noticed that amongst the flock of birds, there was no sign of the Hood-Hood bird (also known as the Hoopoe bird; it has black and white colouring and a fan-like crest).

"Where is my Hood-Hood?" asked the King. "Why has he not come to honour me?" He was very angry indeed and demanded that the Hood-Hood be found and brought to him so that he could be punished. The rest of the birds were sent away to search for the missing Hood-Hood. When they found him, the Hood-Hood was most contrite and immediately hopped to the foot of the King's throne and appealed to him:

"Forgive me your majesty," he pleaded, "I beg you - do not be angry with me. I have been flying around the world for the last

وَتَفَقَّدَ الطَّيْرَ فَقَالَ مَا لِيَ لَا أَرَى الْهُدْهُدَ أَمْ كَانَ مِنَ الْغَائِبِينَ ((صدق الله العظيم))

few months visiting strange, distant lands and I did not hear you call."

"Where have you been that so enchanted you?" asked Solomon sternly. "What fine place have you found that prevents you from heeding the voice of your King?"

The Hood-Hood then went on to tell him of the marvellous country of Sheba: "My Lord," he said, " In Sheba the earth is wonderfully fertile and planted with forests of Cypress trees which have been growing there since the beginning of time. The land is rich in spice and more precious than silver or gold, while the people are gentle and truthful."

The King was impressed by these stories but when the Hood-Hood told him of the beautiful Queen Bilkis who ruled over the land of Sheba, he was astonished to hear that she and her subjects worshipped the sun instead of God.

"How can it be that she does not bless God for all the gifts he has given her?" exclaimed the King. He was shocked to discover that Queen Bilkis did not believe in God. He told the Hood-Hood that

he would forgive him for his absence if he returned to Sheba with a message for the Queen. Of course the Hood-Hood agreed and, carrying the message in his beak, he flew away. The other birds, who were curious about this beautiful, far-off place, followed him, flying across the deserts, mountains and wide oceans until together they reached the land of Sheba.

As the birds approached, the Queen of Sheba was praying. She was bowing down before the morning sun so that when the Hood-Hood and his followers flew overhead they blocked out the light, throwing her into confusion. The Queen was frightened; as she stood up, alarmed by the sudden darkness, the Hood-Hood swooped down and presented her with the letter from King Solomon.

With trembling fingers she opened the letter and read that King Solomon wished to see her. He asked her to come immediately to Jerusalem so that he could tell her about the one true God. Bilkis was worried. What should she do? She spoke to her advisers, but they were afraid that King Solomon would want to conquer their country. They advised her to remain safely at home. However, the Queen knew that Solomon was a powerful King and she tried to

قالت يَا أَيُّهَا الْمَلَأُ إِنِّي أُلْقِيَ إِلَيَّ كِتَابٌ كَرِيمٌ ۝ إِنَّهُ مِن سُلَيْمَانَ وَإِنَّهُ بِسْمِ اللَّهِ الرَّحْمَٰنِ الرَّحِيمِ ﴿صَدَقَ اللهُ العَظيم﴾

think of a way to placate him. She decided to send an ambassador in her place and she asked her loyal subjects to build a fleet of boats which she filled with gold and jewels to take with him.

However, when Solomon received the Queen's generous presents, he was not at all impressed. He was angered that Bilkis had failed to obey him. As he listened to the Hood-Hood's stories describing the Queen's splendid throne, adorned with beautiful carvings and studded with emeralds and rubies, he wondered how he could show her that the powers which God gave him were far greater than hers. He ordered the Jinns to go to Sheba and, with their magic, remove the Queen's precious throne. When this happened, Bilkis knew she had offended him and that it was unwise to disappoint him twice - she had no choice but to go to Jerusalem.

So, eventually the Queen of Sheba set off on the long journey to visit Solomon. She took with her a huge train of camels bearing gold, silver and precious stones. She also carried a great store of spices amongst which was Balsam - the most expensive and highly prized spice in the land. Finally, she brought him a gift of one thousand maidens and boys, all born on the same day of the

قال عفريت من الجن أنا آتيك به قبل أن تقوم من مقامك وإني عليه لقوي أمين. قال الذي عنده علم من الكتاب أنا آتيك به قبل أن يرتد إليك طرفك

same year and all dressed in purple robes.

After three years of travelling she finally arrived in Jerusalem to meet King Solomon. The Jinns saw her procession and marvelled at how beautiful she was. Fearing that the King would fall in love with her and wish to marry her, they spread the rumour that she was not human, but a demon with hairy legs like those of a horse. When Solomon heard this rumour he dismissed it as a terrible lie, but still he could not quite forget what he had been told.

How could he discover the truth? He called the Jinns to him and ordered them to build him a palace of marble, with a floor of transparent glass through which one could see fish swimming in shallow water. He then had his own throne, guarded by wild animals, placed at one end of the palace floor.

When the Queen of Sheba approached Solomon he saw that she was indeed very beautiful. Her skin was the colour of milk and her eyes sparkled like the brightest star in the evening sky. He admired her greatly but he was still concerned by the mischievous stories he had heard from the Jinns.

فَلَمَّا جَاءَتْ قِيلَ أَهَكَذَا عَرْشُكِ قَالَتْ كَأَنَّهُ هُوَ وَأُوتِينَا الْعِلْمَ مِنْ قَبْلِهَا وَكُنَّا مُسْلِمِينَ

He summoned her, asking her to walk across the glass floor and sit next to him. Bilkis looked at the floor and thought that Solomon's throne was set in a lake of water. Imagining that she would have to wade through the water the Queen lifted the hem of her long skirt modestly so that she would not get her dress wet. As she walked towards him, the king was relieved to catch a glimpse of her ankle and see that she had normal feet and smooth legs, and not the hooves of a horse as he had feared!

To punish the Jinns for their lies he made them build a bath-house near the gate at the Bab al-Asbat for the Queen's use. Although the King had cleverly discovered that Bilkis was not a demon - she still worshipped the sun. If he wanted to marry her he would have to convince her to worship God instead.

On the journey the Queen had heard many tales of Solomon's intelligence and wisdom. However, when the King told her about God's greatness, she remained unsure.

"Oh most gracious Lord," she said, "You are known throughout the land as a good, honest, and, above all, wise King - but I wish that you would prove to me that you are not like other men. Show

قيل لها ادخلي الصرح فلما رأته حسبته لجة وكشفت عن ساقيها قال إنه صرح ممرد من قوارير قالت رب إني ظلمت نفسي وأسلمت مع سليمان لله رب العالمين

me your wisdom by answering these three riddles." Solomon was anxious to bring the Queen to the one true God and so he agreed.

The next day the Queen came to Solomon's court and asked him, "Tell me, oh Lord, what is as black as the night, and yet brings daylight to the world?"

Without hesitation Solomon replied, "Oh gentle Queen - of course it is the oil that seeps from the ground and which lights our lamps."

The Queen was impressed and surprised that Solomon had answered so quickly and she returned to her quarters to think of another question.

The next day as she was preparing to meet the King, she brushed her long dark hair, and made up her beautiful eyes. As usual the black kohl made her eyes water as she painted it on. This gave her an idea - surely the King would know nothing of these womanly things. So, when she went before him she asked: "Oh your honoured one - what is as hard as stone and makes us weep with beauty?"

The King looked into the Queen's lovely eyes and knew the answer immediately. "Why, of course it must be kohl," he said and once again the Queen was amazed by his cleverness.

The next question would be her final one and she would have to make it as difficult as possible. That night she thought for a very long time and finally came up with a riddle that surely Solomon would never be able to guess. When she returned to the King's palace she took with her the one thousand boys and girls, all dressed alike in their purple robes and all born on the same day of the same year.

She assembled them in the great throne room. "Oh your gracious majesty," she said, "Can you tell amongst all these young people - which are the boys and which are the maidens?"

This was an impossible question as each of the girls looked exactly like each of the boys. Each child was the same height and the same age and every one wore identical purple clothing. She knew that Solomon could not possibly tell the difference.

Solomon looked at the large throng gathered in front of him and thought for a second. He remembered the first time the Queen had come to see him and how she had thought that the floor was covered in water. This gave him an idea. He called for silence and commanded that each person should walk towards him. After he spoke, the crowd divided. Some of the young people pulled their robes almost to their knees, as if to wade through the water, while others merely lifted their robes to the tips of their ankles. In this way Solomon knew who were the boys and who were the girls - of course the maidens were the modest ones who refused to show their legs.

The Queen was now totally convinced. She said: "I would never have believed it unless I had seen it with my own eyes, but when I heard of your wisdom and goodness, I did not believe it was to such an extent - you truly are a great man!"

The Queen wanted to give King Solomon a special gift to show how highly she regarded him; but he wanted only one thing - that she should become one of the true believers. Bilkis needed no further encouragement so immediately she bowed down and accepted the one true God.

فَمَكَثَ غَيْرَ بَعِيدٍ فَقَالَ أَحَطتُ بِمَا لَمْ تُحِطْ بِهِ وَجِئْتُكَ مِنْ سَبَإٍ بِنَبَإٍ يَقِينٍ ﴿ صدق الله العظيم ﴾

The King was overjoyed that the Queen of Sheba had finally turned her back on worshipping the sun. He proposed to her, and the Queen graciously agreed to be his wife. They now lived together happily for many years. Meanwhile the Hood-Hood - who had found the Queen and who had played such an important part in bringing her to Jerusalem - was from then on given an extra special place in the King's heart.

Heroes From the East

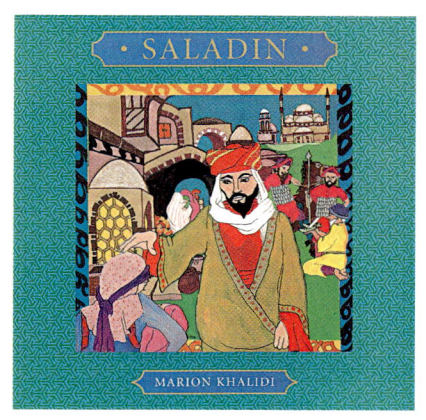

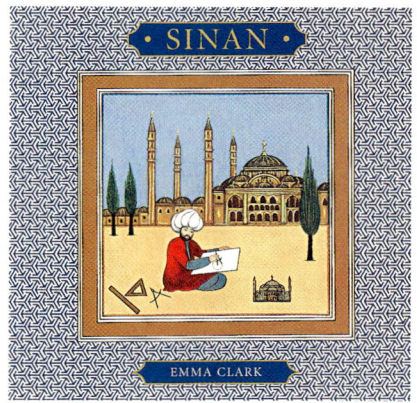

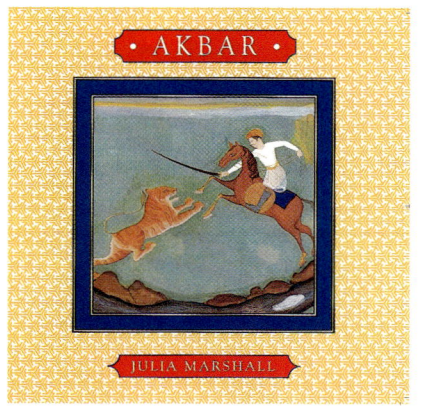

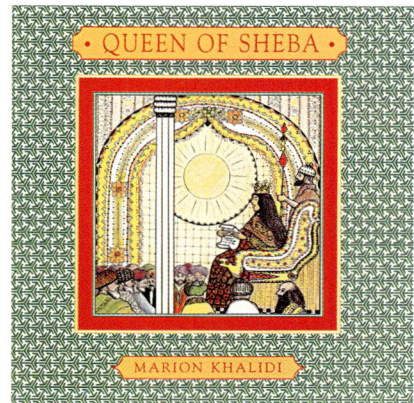